# My Life as a
# TRAVELING HOME-SCHOOLER

## IN THE WORDS OF AN 11-YEAR-OLD

# Jenifer Goldman

SOLOMON PRESS PUBLISHERS
Education Division

The Solomon Press,
Educational Division
417 Roslyn Rd.
Roslyn Hts. NY 11577

Photographs by Jerry Mintz

Cover design by Sidney Solomon

ISBN 0-934623-75-9

Library of Congress Cataloging-in-Publication Data

Goldman, Jenifer, 1979-
    My life as a traveling home schooler : as told by an 11 year old /
Jenifer Goldman.
        p.    cm.
    Summary: The author describes her education under a home school
program, as well as her experiences in public and private schools.
    ISBN 0-934623-75-9
    1. Home schooling--United States--Case studies--Juvenile
literature.  2. Education, Elementary--United States--Case studies-
-Juvenile literature.  [1. Home schooling.  2. Schools.
3. Goldman, Jenifer, 1979-   .  4. Children's writings.]  I. Title.
LC40.G65   1991
649'.68--dc20                                              91-14586
                                                              CIP
                                                               AC

## Dedication

To my Grandpa, Samson Mintz, because he started my interest in reading. I think he would be proud that I used some of the things he taught me to write this book.

# CONTENTS

# I
# Before Homeschooling: Public School

Through most of my life school's been pretty miserable. When I started homeschooling, everything got better. I can't remember much of nursery school or kindergarten, but some of the reasons why I didn't like school were--well, why don't I just give you an example of some of the things that have happened to me?:

I was in fourth grade. I had a teacher named Miss Jay. She was the teacher of my worst nightmares. We were having a vote on who should write the end of the year graduation speech. I suggested to the teacher that we not tell whose paper it was that we were reading, because I figured that some people would do it by who their friend was, rather than whose paper they liked best. They voted my paper the best, so I was selected to do the speech. But the teacher seemed to try anything possible to stop me from doing it.

Three other kids had also tried to write a speech, so the teacher decided that we should all work together. We started working together, but just because I was behind on a couple of papers, she took away the privilege for me to write it, even though I was the one who was selected. The teacher said that I "owed" her work. So the other kids went on to make the speech, and I sat and did extra work. Personally, I thought it was very unfair, because after the kids all decided that mine was the best, the teacher kicked me out of it. I told different people about it, but nobody listened, so that's just what I had to live with.

Most of my education has been through public school, but I also learned from the people in my family. These included my mother, my father, my uncle Jerry, my nana, and my grandpa (until I was seven years old--it's hard to believe that it was three and a half years ago, because I remember him so well, it just seems like a few months). My uncle Jerry is one of the main characters throughout this book, along with me.

My nana's been a big help in many things, such as spelling, math, when I was first learning multiplication, and she also taught me much about piano, because she's a piano teacher.

# *BEFORE HOMESCHOOLING: PUBLIC SCHOOL*

*Me and Nana, standing in front of our house*

*Me with my mother*

Me as a baby with
my Nana and Grandpa

My grandpa took me a lot of places and taught me just about everything, especially reading, because I always used to sit on his lap and he would read books to me. He used to take me to the zoo, to movies, to the playground, and anyplace else that he needed to go.

My father and mother got divorced when I was four, but I see my father once every month. He lives in Cambridge, Mass. My father teaches me a lot about science, and a lot about mechanics, since he had been working for Xerox, and now works for Savin, fixing copying machines. He can fix just about anything. He's taught me a lot about problems with cars and electronic things.

My mother taught me about crafts and sign language, because she's been a special ed teacher in classrooms and an art teacher in summer camps.

I've been living in the same house with my nana and my uncle Jerry for many years, and before that, we used to visit all the time. Jerry taught me many things, and a lot of what I know now. Jerry used to run an alternative school in Vermont. Then Jerry became the director of a company called the NCACS (National Coalition of Alternative Community Schools). So, when I was having trouble in school, Jerry thought that it might be a good idea for me to homeschool for a while.

*Sitting on my uncle Jerry's lap when I was three*

# 2
# The Trip to Niagara Falls and Toronto

That summer I went on my first trip with Jerry. Here's what I wrote about it:

My name is Jenifer and I'm ten years old. I hadn't ever traveled with my Uncle Jerry before. I had heard many stories about my Uncle Jerry's trips. I've always wanted to go on a trip with him.

My uncle said that he thought I could go on this trip with him because he thought I was old enough now. I just turned ten.

He had to go to a meeting in Canada on decentralism. I think that decentralism means not being in a large group all doing the same thing and having one leader telling you what to do all the time.

I decided to go about two days before we were ready to leave. We thought we would go camping somewhere around Niagara Falls so we bought a tent. I had more experience camping than Jerry did, and I had to push him to go camping for at least a night.

We had to have my birth certificate because I was leaving the country, and I had a big fight with my mother to try to get her to give me the original because I didn't think they would accept a copy. This was my first time out of the country.

We left Sunday afternoon. I think we packed a little bit too much stuff, at least I did. First we went over the Throg's Neck Bridge, then the George Washington, which is a double decker. It goes over the Hudson River.

The first city we went to was Albany. We went to visit Chris and his family from the Albany Free School. He had two girls, age five and two.

We got there around 6:00 o'clock. Chris was milking goats at the time, and I thought that that was rather odd for being in a city. He has five goats and he milks two. He showed me how to milk the goats, and I gave it a try. He said I was a fast learner because I got the milk out right away on my first try. I never expected that I would be milking goats especially in the city of Albany.

They also had chickens and ten cats, all wild. They adopted two of them to keep in the house.

Lana, their babysitter, came over that night. My uncle and Chris went out to play tennis. While they were playing tennis, we played games. Lana went to the Albany Free School. Angela came over later. She had gone to the Albany Free School and Shaker Mountain, my uncle's school. Angela was very nice.

*L: These are the jungle gyms in back of Albany's Free School*
*R: A boy and a girl at the Free School in Albany, NY.*

*The sign in front of the Free School*

We slept at Chris' house that night. He gave us a bed and a mattress to sleep on. Jerry took the mattress on the floor because he thought it would be more supportive, and I took the bed.

The next day we milked the goats, played around the house a while, and then left to see Jerry's Uncle Morris and Aunt Hester, my Nana's older sister. We caught Morris just on the way out. He was leaving to play a golf game. We saw him out on the street. We both stopped and got out of our cars to say hello to each other. We then went up to the house, went in, and surprisingly, Aunt Hester had a nice lunch waiting for us. I can see a little bit of Nana in her: She always tried to get in the last word. She was very nice, and she gave us $50 to help with the trip, for us to go to Marineland. We gave her one of our jewelry boxes. She gave us some food for snacks. Then we left and continued on toward Niagara Falls.

We arrived in the area about 10:00 or 10:30. We waited in line to get over the border at least a half hour.

When we first got to the border I was very excited because I knew that as soon as we showed our birth certificate and passport and stuff that we would be in another country. At the border we showed our stuff, and we had no trouble getting in.

When we got over the Rainbow Bridge I saw Niagara Falls for the first time. I thought it was the most beautiful thing that I had ever seen. The colored lights that were shining on the falls made it look even prettier.

We talked about camping out but as we were driving toward the camp ground, Jerry stopped at a motel and he said, "OK campers, follow me, into the motel!" We found out how much it would cost, which was about $40 a night, so I dragged Jerry out and back over the camp ground which fortunately was only $14 a night, and that was in Canadian money.

After we got to the camp ground we checked in and set our tent up which was very simple because we had done it once before in our backyard. I had put the seam sealer on and I hoped it would work.

*I took this one of Jerry in front of
our tent at Niagara Falls*

After we got our tent set up, we went to the downtown area to get something to eat. We went to a restaurant called Mother's and had pizza and spaghetti. Then we walked down the street looking at all the stores and tourist attractions. I thought that it looked really fun, and I hoped that we would be able to come down the next night to go into some of the tourist attractions.

The next morning we went to a breakfast bar for all you can eat. It was breakfast and lunch combined because we were going to be in Marineland all day, and food costs more there.

This is a picture we took of Canada's
Horseshoe Falls at Niagara Falls

At Marineland I went on the big steel roller coaster three times; once in the middle, once in the back, and the last time I waited to get the front. Jerry chickened out and didn't go on it at all. He thought I was real gutsy, especially to get the front seat. The ride was really neat. It had four loops upside down. They said it was the longest steel roller coaster in the world. The ride took about three minutes.

I went on a few other rides that Jerry also chickened out on. I didn't make Jerry go on the rides because I didn't want a sick and grumpy Uncle Jerry for the rest of the time.

Then we did something for both me and Jerry. We went to the King Waldorf show which was sea lions, dolphins and killer whales, all in a big comedy act. The funniest thing was when the killer whale went along the side and whacked the water, splashing people at least ten or twenty rows deep into the audience.

After that, we went to a deer park. We bought some deer food. At first we bought only one cone of it. The deer were all around the food shop, and they wouldn't let you walk away without trying to take the cone out of your hand. Finally we made our way out. We got another cone, and we had a herd of deer following us and jumping at us to try to get the food. Then we tried to get as large a herd as we could over to the other end of the deer park, following us as we fed them. We had 25, and 15 of them stayed with us all the way.

We stayed at Marineland for about five hours altogether. That night we had supper at the Ponderosa and went to some of the tourist attractions including the Guiness Museum of World Records. We saw things like the tallest man, the oldest man. We saw a bird eating a bug, the biggest insect. We saw who sold the most records. For your information, Madonna had one of the most successful records. I bought a couple of souvenir T shirts.

Back at the camp ground we tried to start a camp fire. At first we were having a lot of trouble because we didn't have any kindling. Eventually we got it started. We roasted some marshmallows. We also set off some sparklers that we had bought and one fountain. We had two sparklers left, and there were a couple of kids across the street from us so we went over to them and gave them the sparklers and the rest of our marshmallows. Then the kids and I went over to the park. Meanwhile, Jerry was talking to their parents.

One of the girls had aplastic anemia, and she was waiting for a bone marrow transplant. Every two days she had to have a blood transfusion. I felt really bad for her.

After I went swimming we took down the tent and headed for Toronto. When we got there we went to Jerry's friend, Satu Repo's house. We met her daughter, Lisa, who had just been in a big Canadian movie. It was a sequel, and she played the friend of the star. The star thought that she was taking over the show. She said that she got paid $28,000 to be in the movie. She is 18 years old now. She is very pretty, and I can see why they chose her.

After that we went to a woman's rights rally with Satu. Then we went to a diner with her. Then it was our turn to take her to our meeting. The main speaker was Ivan Ilich.   I thought it was really dull and boring.    I didn't understand anything except the "and's" and the "the's."    Even if I do have a good vocabulary, this was ridiculous.    So I drew some pictures of boats on the water, and I used origami boats and used pipe cleaners to hold them in place.

We stayed at Satu's place and met her kitty cats. For the next couple of days we kept going to the conference and staying at Satu's house at night.

Satu Repo          Me with Lisa, the girl who was in the movie

One day we went to the Royal Ontario Museum. The Egyptian exhibit was pretty stinky compared to the Metropolitan, but I loved the dinosaurs.

One night we were supposed to meet the rest of the group at a deli called "Druxy's."   We went there, talked a while, and then they decided to go to a pub. We all left, but very appropriately for a decentralist meeting, we lost our leader along the way.   He went down Bloor Street but the leader of the rest of the group decided to go straight so we followed him to a

pub called "The Idler" which was very far away, and
my feet were killing me by the time we got there. It
was really nice there, and everybody was telling
funny jokes and stories. One guy sang the "Popeye"
song in German, and Jerry sang "Row, Row, Row Your
Boat" backwards. Then John Papworth, from England,
recited "The Highwayman." He was the one who
started the organization. Somebody on the street
once described him as a "pleasantly cranky old man,"
which we thought was very funny but we didn't think
he would like it.

After we left the conference on Saturday, we went

One night Jerry did his presentation, and showed
his alternative schools tape. The next day some of the
people had a meeting with Jerry about having him
work for them. I did my own workshop, teaching
origami to the younger kids that were there.

After we left the conference on Saturday, we went
to the CNN Tower, which has the highest observation
deck in the world. We went all the way up to the top,
which was 140 stories high! It was amazing. You
could see the whole city of Toronto, and we saw a
clipper ship in the harbor, and we found our car,
which was really amazing.

*A view from the CNN Tower in Toronto, the tallest observation
deck in the world (140 stories up)*

*A picture I took of Jerry at the top of the CNN Tower.*
*Right: Me at the top of the CNN Tower*

We cut through a convention center on the way back to our car, and found ourselves in the music convention, which most people probably paid to get into, and they were demonstrating to the people how to write a song in one of the meetings. They were using an electronic synthesizer to write the music for the song.

Then we drove back to Niagara Falls and we went to the Maid of the Mist. It is a tour boat which goes under the falls, and of course, supplies you with rain coats. It was really cool on the Maid of the Mist. When we went by the American Falls we saw a rainbow, but we didn't get very wet. We went up to the Canadian Horseshoe Falls, into the very center, and kept on moving until we were so close to the falls that we thought it was going to come down right on our heads.

We set up our tent at the KOA, real luxury camping. They had an indoor swimming pool, cold and hot whirlpools, a steam room, an arcade, and showed videos at night. They also had an outdoor pool with a diving board. They had a miniature golf

16

course, which we played the next morning. I did
fairly well. Jerry beat me by ten points, but I got the
only hole in one.

For our last breakfast in Canada we had crepes,
and I called them "creeps," but they were good. Then
we went back across the border, but I didn't want to
go back. There was about a half hour of traffic
because it was Sunday and a lot of people were going
back to the United States. We had no trouble getting
across the border. They didn't even check our papers.
Jerry said that it is sometimes harder getting back
into the United States, but it turned to to be easier.

# 3

# I Tried A Private School

Later that summer, we looked into starting an alternative school in the area. I went to a few meetings with this group called the Learning Tree. They used to have an alternative school and were thinking about starting it up again. We talked about how we would run it and what kind of democracy there would be, and how the students would be able to vote in the meetings. But we never ended up starting the school.

So we decided that I should try a school more toward an alternative school. It was a private school called Berrywood Friends. It was a Quaker school (although there weren't any Quakers in it).

At first I was enjoying it there. It was quiet. There were much fewer kids in one classroom. I thought that I was going to do a lot better there. In the end, I still thought I did. But there was something wrong. I'm still not sure what it was.

The kids there were either much too calm--they never did anything but sit around and talk or make string bracelets, or the kids were all running around hitting kids or being mean, which wasn't right for me, either. So after a while, we agreed that it would be best if I left there and tried something new.

After that I went back to public school, because I had no place else to go.

# 4
# Trip to New York for TV Show, Pictures

W hile I was back in public school,   Jerry helped me find a manager because I wanted to get into acting. He brought me to a mall for a tryout, and they picked me and two others out of about 200 kids. This is story about a day when I went in to have pictures taken:

In February of 1990 I was called into New York City by my manager. He was a manager for theater, television shows and commercials. He said I needed pictures if I ever wanted to get an acting job, because he needed to show them my picture.

That same day, Jerry was scheduled to be on a TV show. He was going to talk about homeschooling and alternative education on a   show called "Best Talk on Location" on channel 11. It was going to be taped at an   alternative   school   called   Manhattan   Country School.

We got there by taking a train and two subways.

At first, the school looked like a plain old brick building, but, boy, it wasn't. Inside, it was big, roomy, and very friendly. In the back there was an area that was outside, but with walls around it, for basketball and other games.

Then we went into this big room where we started getting ready for taping. They put a microphone on Jerry, put these blue things over the lights, I think they call them gels, and aimed them at us until it was blinding.

Then they started taping. Jerry talked about all sorts of stuff, including alternative education, homeschooling, and me.

They also interviewed the guy who ran the school. He talked about the way he had designed the school to have just as many blacks as whites. They had a sliding scale for tuition. That way everyone could afford to go there.

Afterwards, we went outside, and they had me do the promo to the show that Jerry was on, to let people know what was going to be on the next show. They had me memorize a short line, and I had to do it about five times before I got it right.

When this was all done, we went to have my picture taken. First, they had me pick out the outfit I was going to wear. Then, they put a lot of makeup on me, including blush, base creme, and a lot of other goop. The photographer took a whole lot of pictures, at least two rolls.

Out of the 74 pictures he took, they selected one to be my acting picture. That one they enlarged and made 100 copies, and that's the picture at the end of this chapter.

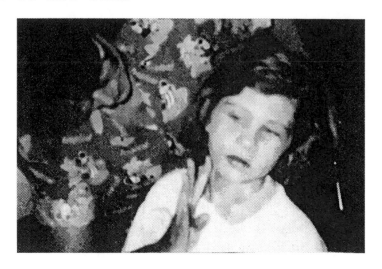

L Getting makeup put on when I was
having my professional picture taken

Uncle Jerry when he was getting
ready for his TV show

This was my publicity picture

JENIFER GOLDMAN

# 5
# More Public School Problems

I didn't do too well when I went back to the public school again. I mean, I was starting in the middle of the year, and the kids who knew me thought something was wrong because I was gone for so long. They were overloading me with homework. I would sit there and work on it, and if I even took a small break, I wouldn't get it done in time. Sometimes I would stay up until midnight, trying to do the homework. Then they said, since I wasn't getting my work done, I would have to stay after school to do it. Every day after school I would go to the principal's office, sit at a desk, and work on my homework. Fifteen minutes before the late bus came, I was let out. Then I'd get on the late bus, go home, and work on my homework again. Sometimes, I'd sit in bed, working on it. Other times, I just wouldn't get it done.

Sometimes the teacher gave me extra work when my homework wasn't done. That, I thought, was silly. Because, if I couldn't get my work done in the first place, why give me more?

Then they decided that they wanted to do some testing on me, because they thought that something was wrong. I thought that if I passed it it would be good, but if I messed up at all, then they might do something bad.

Jerry suggested that maybe we could try homeschooling for a few months. I thought it was a good idea, but we had a time trying to get my mom and dad to agree. Finally, we decided that I would try it, for just a few months.

I first found out that I was going to be able to homeschool when I went on a trip with Jerry to Virginia and the NCACS (alternative schools) conference. We decided to take notes and keep a log of all my homeschool experiences, which is what this is from here on.

# 6
# NCACS Trip to Virginia:
# I Start Homeschooling

This is the kind of thing that is very hard to describe, but I felt that I was taking in a lot of information. I learned a lot.

The first night, one of the first things that I did was help them set up the (conference) store. One of the adults came up to Jerry and was talking to him, and then asked me if I wanted to help out with the store. Her name was Faye, and she has a son, Stewart, who is home schooling.

I priced the items in the store, and then set it up, and sold them. I went around looking for some other kids to help with the store. It turned out that I found two other kids to help. The name of one of them was

Sasha. I think her real name is Cristy, but she likes to be called Sasha. Sasha is her middle name. The other one was a younger kid, seven years old. Her name was Courtney. She came from Chicago, and her mother teaches at Dupage Community School. The store went pretty well and I think we made a lot of money. The first night we made $50.

Another thing that I had to do was tell Josh the things that we were running out of that we needed to order. Josh was the adult who was in charge of the store (he is 17). he wasn't always around, but he'd stop by every once in a while to pick up the cash box and to pack the stuff up.

Some of the people questioned the prices, especially since we had to take the tags off of the things that had been bought and raise the prices a little bit. We had to explain to them that we had to make a profit, and we certainly didn't want to take a loss, and that the money was going to the Coalition.

While running the store I met a lot of new people and made a lot of new friends.

At one point we moved the store from the dining hall down to the arts and crafts center. On the way walking down there I met a couple of kids from another school and I became friends with them, too. They were doing something really funny when I met them. They were pouring water over a kid's head and putting it in pony tails all over. It turned out that they were going to do a crazy barber act at the talent show. So they asked my new friend and I if we wanted to join the act. We said yes.

We had a day to practice for the talent show. Then we went down and signed up for it and got right to rehearsal. Meanwhile, this kid was getting ready to kill, us because he was getting soaking wet.

Now the big night was coming close. We were getting all our props ready. We were just doing it ourselves. I came up with half of the lines and they came up with the other half.

Now it was time for us to go up on stage. A couple of them were a little nervous, but I wasn't. I think it went pretty well.

A few girls who were in my cabin did a dancing act. I think their act was probably the best one that night.

Speaking of my cabin, it was really nice. There were mostly girls from the Farm School. The only two boys in the cabin were two of the fathers of the girls. Jerry's cabin was next door. Our cabin was heated, one of the only three. I felt sorry for Jerry, who had to sleep in the cold one.

One of the girls in the cabin had a pet mouse. Her mother didn't know it was hers. She kept it in a suitcase and fed it hamster food. She told her mother it was her friend's mouse. Most of the kids in the cabin were really pretty nice.

The food was very good, even though it was mostly vegetarian, and I'm not used to it. We had to bring our own dishes and wash them ourselves. This wasn't anything new for me, because when I went to girl scout camp we had to do the same thing. The reason why we did that was because we didn't want to produce a lot of garbage.

I went down to the lake. I felt sort of like I was at the creek in my old house in Pennsylvania, except it was a lot bigger. There were little tiny peeper frogs and sunfish. We saw one of the park ranger's husbands fishing. He let each of us try to cast the line. After that he caught a sunfish, and he let me release it. He wasn't going to keep it because he was only fishing for fun. He had to hold the fish a special way because it has sharp points on the top to protect it. I saw a really big bat flying over the lake, and the ranger's husband said they had spotted an eagle right at that site. So we waited to see if we could find it, but it didn't come.

The ranger, who was his wife, came into the lunch room, at dinner time, to make an announcement. She said that we were one of the cleanest groups that she had ever seen. She said that the group before us had made a big mess. She even bought a tie die shirt from us. John Iber, who was selling the shirts, told the story of the ranger when she came over: She said, "You know, those cars aren't supposed to be parked there--and how much is that shirt?" And then she bought it.

On the second day of the conference we went into Washington, DC on four coach busses. We were going to see our congressmen and go to see museums. We were going to see our congressmen to tell them about alternative education. The first thing that we did was we went to a couple of senators' offices. They weren't in, but we left them information. From Senator Moynahan's office we got passes to go into the Senate. The Senate is one of the places where they make all the laws, and we got to see a meeting in session. It turned out to not be very important, but it was worth it just to see where it happens. In order to have a law passed, both the House of Representatives and the Senate have to pass it and agree. The reason why there are two lawmakers is because the smaller states didn't want to join the United States because they were afraid that the bigger states would overrule them when they voted. So they said that the smaller states and the bigger states would each have two

Senators, and that the Representatives would be by population and they would both have to pass it.

After leaving Moynahan's office, we went over to the offices for the House of Representatives in order to try to see Jerry's friend, Peter Smith, who is a representative of Vermont, (Vermont doesn't have many people, so it only gets one representative). They both were starting alternative schools in Vermont at the same time. That's how Jerry knew him. At first his secretary said, "You won't be able to see him. He's in meetings all day." So Jerry said, "Would you at least tell him that I'm here?" and he said to me, "I bet he'll come out." I didn't think he would, but Jerry guaranteed me. And guess what? A couple of minutes later he opened the door and saw Jerry sitting there. He ran out and gave Jerry a big hug. I'm sure that he's the only one who got a hug from his congressman that day.

After that we went to the Capitol. We went to the dome. It was really pretty. It was so big that just looking up could make you dizzy. It's the largest cast iron dome in the world. It's over 100 years old.

*Me at the Botanical Gardens in Washington, DC*

Looking up at the Capitol Dome in Washington, DC

Then we went to the botanical gardens. The flowers there were really pretty, and I enjoyed it a lot. There was a palm tree that almost busted through the ceiling. I liked the Sweet Williams. We also saw orchids . I'm only naming the best part.

Then we went to the Natural History Museum. We saw some dinosaur bones and the largest blue diamond in the world. Then we went to the Air and Space museum to see a movie. It was in the OMNI Theater, which is a theater with a five story high screen, which curved, and makes some people dizzy. The movie was about people going up in outer space.

At the conference, Jerry and I had a really good system: He'd put me to bed at night, and I'd wake him up in the morning. Sometimes he was hard to wake up, but I'd do it anyway, because I knew he wouldn't want to miss breakfast.

One night we had an auction to raise money for the Coalition. Jerry was the auctioneer, and I was a runner. It was the first time I had ever seen Jerry do an auction. It went  well. We earned about $600.

I went to a few of the workshops. One was origami. I didn't learn anything new, because I do a lot of origami myself, but I helped some people do their origami. I also helped Jerry with his temporary tattoo workshop. We each held one line and painted them on and helped the kids learn how to do it. I also went with a group that was playing ultimate frisbee. It was pretty much the way I play frisbee normally: Every time you miss it the other team gets a point.

I really enjoyed this trip. It gave me a chance to feel what it was like to have freedom. To me, freedom means a chance to make your own decisions. It's not just that you have to respect other people's rights.

Even without freedom you have to respect other people's rights. But I felt that my right to make decisions was being respected also.

The kids there seemed to be more like me, and I was able to get along with them. Whenever I go to other places, kids are always so concerned about fashion, and I have to look exactly right, or I don't fit in. Here, I still wanted to look good, but I felt that I didn't have to be so worried whether I looked perfect or not. I feel that we were treated more fairly, and kids were treating each other more fairly. Their whole attitude toward life and what it means was different. They didn't believe in violence. They didn't exclude other kids because of their race or color. Their overall view seemed a lot　　better.

Finally the day came that we had to leave. I didn't enjoy having to leave, but it was just as well, because I couldn't spend the rest of my life there.

*This is me telling the squirrel that I have no food*

# 7
# Question Class

One of the first things we did when we got back home was a question class, where Jerry asked me to just brainstorm any questions that came to my mind. Then I rated the ones I was most interested in, and we studied those first. These were the questions we came up with. The numbers are my rating, on a scale of ten. It took about a half hour.

What's the point of this? 7

How does a TV Work? 5

How did life on Earth start? 6

Why are kids mean to me? 8
Who invented the lamp shade? 5

Who thought of putting pockets in pants? Who invented the zipper? Buttons? 7

Who invented the belt?

Who invented the computer? Who invented the Mouse. Who invented the name Apple? How come Apple and Macintosh are related (I don't think they even meant it))? 8

Who invented the cellular phone, answering machine? 7

Why doesn't my father live closer to me? 8

Who built the first house on Earth? 7

Why can't people get along more easily? 8

Who invented the piano? (Is that science or music?) 7

Who invented written music? Who was the first person to write music for the piano? 7

Who invented the desk, the table? 7

How can I make more friends? 7

Why don't I like to use the left hand in piano (I know the answer a little bit)? 6

Why do I dislike my art work, and other people always like it? 6

Who wrote the first map? 7

Who thought of having a leader for the first time? When did it first happen, in towns, cities, states, etc.? 8

Why did people start wearing make-up? 6

Where did the first languages come from? If they couldn't communicate with each other, how could they tell people what they meant? 8

Who was the first rock and roll group? 8 How much do electric guitars cost these days? 7

Who was the first farmer? 8

Why are all these questions "who was"? 7

How come most grown-ups never understand us kids? (You notice I say "most") 7

How come kids don't understand us kids, sometimes? 7

How come whenever deep down I'm getting tired of someone, I lose their phone number, and I don't even mean to? 7

How come there isn't life on other planets? 8

How come it appears that we know so much about outer space and we really know so little? 7

How is it possible that the universe is unlimited? It seems impossible. There's got to be some point at which it stops. 8

How come people believe in different religions and they have to be separated because of that?    7

How can I make more friends? How come I have so much trouble making friends in the first place? I don't think I'm so different from other people who are popular? What have I done wrong? 8

Who ever thought of having fun? 7

Who has time to have fun now anyway?7
That's all I can think of.

# 8

# BOOK REPORT ON "PANATI'S EXTRAORDINARY ORIGINS OF EVERYDAY THINGS."

I read a book called "Panati's Extraordinary Origins of Everyday Things." It explains where many ordinary things originated.

Jerry ran a question class for me. Most of the questions I asked were,"Where does it come from?" So Jerry got this book which answers some of the questions I asked. I've learned a lot from it.

For example, do you know why men's and woman's clothes are buttoned differently? It's because men used to dress themselves and woman used to have people dress them. Ever since, woman have had to button their clothing backwards. Did you know that the first decorative buttons were made in 2000 B.C. or that they weren't used as fasteners until the 1200's?

I really enjoyed this book.

# 9
# Meeting With
# The Long Island
# Homeschoolers

At this time, we've been homeschooling for about a month and a half. Overall, I've enjoyed it a lot and had many good experiences.

I can't explain what kind of day today was in one sentence, because it was so confusing. It feels like all the good times and all the bad times in my life just mixed together in a milkshake.

Today we went to a fish hatchery, where I met the group of the Long Island homeschoolers for the first time. Although I had a good time, and the kids that I met were very nice to me, I think that that triggered some bad feelings, because at that point I realized that kids, even Long Island kids, can be nice. And, if all this time they could be nice, why weren't they?

A little while after we got home, I was watching TV. I got into an argument with Jerry over who got to watch the TV at that point. That sounds funny: I got into an argument with Jerry about watching TV. He almost never watches TV.

Jerry called a family meeting, which at that time was Jerry, myself, and Nana. Jerry felt disrespected because he had just let me watch my show, and I wouldn't let him watch afterwards. (Actually, I did let him watch, but I left the room mad). I think the reason that I was acting that way was not because of what happened then, but because of something that had happened in the past:

After I would get home from public school, I wanted to just go in and relax    watch some TV because I was sick and tired of the DARN school (I have an urge to use plenty of other words, but I won't). I'd walk into the den and see Jerry watching TV. I'd say, "Jerry, I'm tired from school and I want to watch TV." He'd say, "No, I'm sorry, I'm watching something right now." Another situation would come up in which I would be watching TV, and Jerry would want to watch something. Usually, Jerry is very understanding, so this is a situation that is unusual But he would come in and say, "I want to watch something," and start watching it, without paying attention to whether I was in the middle of a show. So in away, I was angry because of what had happened before, not what happened tonight.

Thinking about that brought out some other bad feelings. At one point in the meeting Jerry had summarized the point that I had made in the meeting, which I felt that he understood. Then he asked me to explain his point of view.

In the process of explaining it, in a way, I made fun of it. After that, he sort of went up in a small rage, and he said, "You know, my stomach just went like THIS when you said that," and he moved his hands up like he was about to vomit. At that point, I ran out of the room, crying, and went up to my room.

A little while later I came back down,  and Jerry was sitting on the couch, trying to have a meeting with nobody in it. He said, "It's rather hard having a meeting by myself." So I walked back over and joined him. Then I explained to him why I got so angry:

I told him that if I went into a rage like that in my school, which built up a lot of rage in me, I would probably get detention for three weeks, which would make me even more angry. So I would hold it back, trying not to get detention. I kept holding more and more back, until I had to let a little bit of it out. I got a detention, which built up yet more anger.

Try to imagine what it would be like if you got angry like that every time a kid made fun of you. Just think what would happen if I expressed my anger like that every time everyone made fun of me. And it used to happen AT LEAST five times a day, when I was in  school. They would find these little tiny things and make them into big things. Like, "She's got a spot of mud on her shoe." Or, "She has a knot on the end of one of her hairs." Or, "When she was in a race in gym, and she tripped over her own foot."

This meeting brought all those memories back. So today, when I realized that kids could be nice to me, I still wonder, why weren't they?

Long Island Homeschoolers at the Fish Hatchery

L:A turtle at the fish hatchery. **R:**Two little
Long Island Homeschoolers hugging each other

L:Homeschoolers chasing a ball   R:Me and the Long
Island Homeschoolers trying to sail a remote control
boat at the fish hatchery

# 10
# TRIP TO HECKSHER PARK AND THE WHALING MUSEUM

Today Jerry and I went to a homeschoolers' meeting at Hecksher Park in Huntington. They said they were meeting on a hill opposite the stage. We looked around for a while and we couldn't find them. Finally we found one group, well, actually, one person. The girl's name was Anna, and she was almost nine years old. They didn't bring any lunch, so her mother went to a store, down on the corner, to get some food, and Anna and I played.

We took a walk with Jerry because we saw a sign that said, "Corn for feeding ducks," but we couldn't find it. We went into a building, and they said that there wasn't any, and the sign shouldn't be there any more. We found this little flock of goslings and their mother and father. we tip toed up behind them and Jerry touched one on the back. Then we came back, and Anna and I went on the playground and waited for her mother.

The lady at the building we went to said there was a corner store, and at the store they sold cracked corn for the ducks. When Anna's mother got back, we talked about going down to the corner store. Her mother said it was too bad, because if she knew that they didn't give it away there any more, she would have brought some from her house. We were going to go back to the corner store, but Anna's mother realized that they had to go. They left, and so did we.

As we left, Jerry said, "I think there's a whaling museum around here. Why do we see if we can find out where it is?" So we asked a few people, and we found it. The admission price was $3 for both of us together.

We went into the museum and walked around. Jerry was pretty amazed at some of the things that were there. For example, we found out that the largest dinosaur in the world could fit into a blue whale's mouth on his tippy toes, if the whale opens his mouth wide. And a whale's heart is as big as a Volkswagon, and a whale has enough blood to fill an oil truck. And a whale's voice can be heard for hundred's of miles. And plankton is both animal and plant, and not only plant, like Jerry thought. And that a whale eats 10,000 pounds of krill every day.

We listened to the sounds that a whale made. We looked at the gift shop for a while. Then we walked over to another area where they had some exhibits that they were working on. But they had an old bottle, and Jerry said that he had a collection. I said that I had one that I found washed up on the beach. He said that he could probably tell me how old it was. He said that the way you could tell was by looking at the seam line, because a long time ago they used to make bottles by hand. As they used more and more mechanical things on them, the seam line got longer and longer. You can tell if it's a bottle of today if the line goes all the way to the top of the bottle.

We also saw scrimshaw, which is carving that the whalers did in whale bones and tusks. But they can't do that any more, and I'm glad that they can't, because I don't want them to kill the whales for it. There was whaling for many years, and it was an important for them many years ago. Fortunately, now we have substitutes for whale oil and whale blubber, etc.

Then we left. The homeschoolers at the park were only vegetarian and wouldn't eat meat, poultry and fish, and they wouldn't eat dairy products, so we were talking about what ice cream they would be allowed to have. We talked about the soy bean ice cream that the Farm made in Tennessee, so on the way back we stopped at a health food store and got some soy ice cream.

I tasted the ice cream and I didn't like it at all. But I liked the one which Jerry had, which was "rice cream".

L: Long Island Homeschoolers visiting a fishing boat
R:The captain of the fishing boat, lowering his net

# 11
# Montana Trip Notes

I had never even seen the outside of an AMTRACK train, except on a commercial. When I went inside, I explored the train for a while, and it's really amazing. They have a restaurant, the dining car, and it's almost like Bob's Big Boys, or something. The food is pretty good, and there's some really nice people. There's a lounge car where you can go to play cards, or buy snacks at the snack bar. On the Western train, they show movies each night in the lounge car. Some of the movies were "Uncle Buck", "Bat Man", "Cookie", "When Harry Met Sally", and they showed one of the old cartoons, "Top Cat." The Eastern trains are pretty small, but the Western trains are huge double deckers, and they're a lot more fancy. They don't show movies on the Eastern trains, but the Eastern trains are still comfortable to sleep in.

It was pretty comfortable to sleep on the train, although you had to sleep sitting up. The seats leaned back, but not very far. The only trouble with the

Western trains was that they had a bar between the seats, so that, even if you got a double-seater, you had a bar on your back when you tried to lay down.

Some of the things we studied on the train were geography, studying the states that we traveled through on the train, math work book (Jerry helped me work on multiplying fractions, symmetry, and volume). In current events, we looked in the paper and read articles about apartheid in South Africa, Mohawk Indian History (the gambling problem on the Reservation--I read some of it, so it was also reading). Jerry taught me a card game called "Pig", and he says it's a lesson in observation, because when someone gets four of the same cards, they touch their nose, and you have to notice it first. We worked on vocabulary and spelling--we did crossword puzzles, about five of them. We did economics, looking in the stock market--Jerry had bought stock in Telephonos de Mexico, which is a Mexican telephone company. I learned how to look up the stock. I read some things in the "Unusual Origins of Everyday Things" book, about superstitions, such as black cats, "knock on wood", crossed fingers, "God bless you", sneezes, hot dogs, and wedding rings. In current events, we also read about how bears are being threatened, being hunted for their claws and their gall bladders, that the Japanese treasure dearly. We read about "Chorus Line", and its last production, which was also economics because we talked about how much money it took in. That night I took my "New Kids" book and read for a while. So, you see, in the first two days of the trip we did quite a lot, while we were on the train.

L:Taken from the train of a paddle boat on the
Mississippi          R: Snowy mountains in Montana

The sun shining through the
clouds in North Dakota

*The train station in Whitefish, Montana*

We got to Whitefish (Montana) on Wednesday, about midnight. Then we got driven down to Missoula by Liz and John Rantz. By the time we arrived there is was about three O' Clock in the morning.

That morning, I got introduced to two of the four boys that lived there, Caleb and Nathan. Jerry went to a newspaper interview, but I chose not to come with him, because I wanted to stay back and get used to the place. Then we went to visit Sussex, the alternative school there. There were 325 people on the waiting list, and we had to organize another school to put them in. So we went to see Sussex to see how they did it there. I thought it was pretty nice, and the kids showed interest in the things they were doing.

When we were at Sussex, Jerry introduced me to a third boy from the family that we were staying with, Jonah. He doesn't go to Sussex. His father just picked him up and brought him there.

*Me and Nathan having a water fight at Sussex School*

I talked to some of the kids that went to Sussex, and I went inside and talked to one of the teachers. I thought that the teacher seemed pretty nice and pretty generous to the kids. At that point of the day she was having the kids come in, teaching them spin art. A little later we went outside, and there was a guy who was teaching Russian to some of the kids. He was sitting up on the jungle gym, so we sat on the tires and listened in for a while. It was pretty interesting. He was telling Russian folk tales and teaching some Russian words. While I was doing that, Jerry was inside teaching a class to the kids.

Jerry had a meeting that night, and the meeting went pretty well. There were quite a few people. There were at least a hundred, or maybe even more. The purpose of the meeting was to see who was interested in starting a new school.

The next day we went to a nearby park, where they were having a homeschoolers meeting. They had a spelling bee, and I entered in the 5th-8th grade contest. I messed up on my sixth word. I don't remember what the word was, but I remember that the reason why I messed up was because I said "ou" and it was only supposed to be "o".

*Me with some Montana homeschoolers having a spelling bee*

That night we had the first meeting of the people who were really interested in starting a school. It was at a church that said that they would let us meet there. The first thing that Jerry did was call the children up to the front of the room, and we formed a circle. We were going to attempt to have the first meeting of the new school.

I was the chairperson, and the girl sitting across from me kept the log. I thought that the meeting went pretty well, considering that it was the first meeting, and the kids didn't even know each other.

We talked about "rules" and "interests", and "parental supervision." We decided on a new way to vote. That was my idea: Two thirds of the people would have to vote on something in order for it to pass, like majority, but it had to be higher than majority. Also, the others, the minority, if they felt strongly enough, could call a revote. And that passed.

After that, we talked about what kids were interested in, and what they wanted to learn. A lot of kids were interested in math. Some of them said "recess". One of the kids was relating everything to his public school, and trying to make everything like his public school. So I asked him why he was relating everything to his public school, and not what he felt and he wanted. He said, "That's the only thing I have to relate it to."

We adjourned the meeting to the next day, and the kids went outside to play, while they showed a video, "Why do These Kids Love School?", and talked.

The next morning, we had the other meeting, which was really a continuation of the first one. Before the meeting, the kids were all outside playing while the adults talked. One of the kids climbed up on the roof. Some other kids climbed trees, and I was one of them. That was the only thing  to do. Then Jerry came out and saw the kid on the roof and told him to get down, and it was time to have the meeting.

We went inside to the meeting. There was a big circle of chairs in the front of the room: all the kids got in that, and a circle around for the adults.

The meeting started. We continued the same agenda that we started at the last meeting. One of the kids brought up consensus, but it didn't pass.

Another thing on the agenda was "roof". The kid who was up on the roof earlier looked at him strangely. He was the log keeper. He  looked at me and said, "What is that supposed to mean?" He was hoping that it didn't mean what he thought it did. So I told him to move it down from the last thing on the list down to the second thing, so that we could get it over with.

We had a long discussion about that and finally decided that we wouldn't be allowed on the roof. Then, another kid brought up "climbing trees", because he didn't think that the church would like it, and if someone got hurt, the church would have to pay. At that point I thought he was the stupidest and the worst kid in the world. At first, I kept on objecting to not being allowed to climb on the trees, which was what he brought up. Then Jerry looked at me with this funny look, and in the last vote I abstained, because we had decided that me and the other kids who wanted to climb trees could go down to the park, and we could climb trees there. After the meeting, Jerry said, "I'm glad you abstained. I would have been upset if you objected." Later on, we did go to the park and climb trees.

When we came back a little later, Jerry pulled us aside in a little room, and all the kids went in, and we tried to decide on a name for the school. We came up with a lot of things like Bitterroot, Grizzly Bear, Ponderosa, and Shiny Mountain. Then we went out into the big meeting, with the adults included. The adults put about thirty two other names into it. One of the people asked the eight year old kid who thought of the name why he put out "Shiny Mountain". He said, "Because that is one of the nick-names of the state." So someone said, well if that's what it is, it should be "ShinING mountain, rather than ShinY Mountain.". The boy said he had no objections to making the change. Then we voted on all of the names, got it down to ten, and then to four. Finally, we had the last two, which were Ponderosa and Shining Mountain. After the kid explained why he liked the name, a lot of the people changed their mind and started to like that, and finally, Shining Mountain won! So now the name of the school is going to be Shining Mountain School. Hopefully, it will be starting this fall.

*This is the boy who thought of the name*
*of Shining Mountain School*

After the meeting, Jerry's friend, Jerry Nichols, came to pick us up in a pick-up truck. He used to work at Jerry's School. He took us to his house in Stevensville, where he has 130 acres of property. We met his wife, Lisa, and their one year old daughter, and their twelve year old son, William. He LIKES to be called William. Most people never call me by my full name unless they're angry at me.

Jerry Nichols writes legal papers to save the trees. He stops people from cutting down large areas of trees in the wilderness areas. On the way to his house, he took us to a wildlife preserve, where we saw a lot of deer.

The next morning I took a walk into the hills with William. We saw a magpie nest. It had four babies in it.

Later on, before we were going to leave, we went down in a big Jeep called Frankenstein to see a neighbor. William showed me a tree where he had shot a porcupine, and we finally found the dead body. It smelled. Then we walked a little ways away, and we saw an old dried up well. We wanted to see how deep it was. So we took a small rock and dropped it down, and it took about five seconds to reach bottom. Then we found this really long rubber tube, held on to one end and put the other end down the well, and it still didn't reach bottom(Jerry told us later we could figure out how deep it was by using the formula for how fast it goes--32 feet per second per second, and how long it took to hit bottom.) .

*Jerry Nichols at his ranch in Montana*

This is a lake in Montana near where the Nichols' live

*William, Lisa Nichols, and Lisa's new baby*

Then Lisa drove us back to Missoula, and William went with us for the ride.

The next day, we went back to Sussex School again and Jerry talked to the class. We did a question class, which is where you say any question that you want to know the answer to, no matter how stupid it is. One of the questions that Jerry told us some kid asked was, "Do fish fart?" I thought that was pretty funny. Some kids asked questions like, "Do deja vus really happen and why? One of the ones we wound up discussing was, "What is beyond space?" Jerry started explaining Einstein's theory--$E=MC$ squared. I thought it was pretty interesting, especially the part about time slowing down as you get faster.

In the afternoon we went to see Jonah's school, which was St. Joseph's Catholic School (Jonah is the oldest boy in the family that we stayed with. He is almost 10). We showed a couple of videos.

The next morning we went to Clark's Fork School, which is where Stevie went to school. He was the youngest in the family, which I forgot to mention. He is four and a half. It is an alternative school for kids in pre-school and kindergarten. It was a nice school. They had a hamster and a rabbit. I was watching some kids in one room, and Jerry went into the other room. The kids that I was watching were naming things in the picture that they saw, matching things that they put on one paper, and using stickers to duplicate the thing on another paper.

A woman who was interested in teaching at the new school came to pick us up, to bring us where we were going to stay that night, which was in Kalaispiel, which was near the train station. We needed to get close to the train station, because the train was going to leave at five in the morning.

On the way up we stopped at the Flathead Indian Reservation, to look at a shop, and to go into a "casino" where we played a couple of games.

When we got to the house where we were going to stay, there were a couple of kids living there: Josh and Maria. They used to be home schoolers, but not any more. Now they go to public school.

We got up early the next morning and went to the train station. the train was two hours late. So we got on the train. There's not much to say until we got to the last night. The last night we met two kids. They were brother and sister, about 13 and sixteen. They were traveling on their own, going to see their grandparents. We played games and talked and ate until 2 in the morning. I don't think they would have been up until 2 if their parents were there. we decided to stay up because we could sleep late the next morning.

The next afternoon we arrived in Philadelphia station, two hours late. They said we had twenty minutes in the station, so we decided to get off the train to get a snack and make a phone call. We came back in about fifteen minutes, and the train was gone. When we found out that the train had left, our first reaction was, "Oh, no! What are we going to do now?" Our baggage was on the train that we were supposed to be on, going to New York. I wished we could say the same for ourselves.

We went to ask the people at the information booth what we should do. They said that there was another train leaving for New York soon, and they could write us a pass so we could get on it.

We found the train and got on. That train wound up in New York just in time to catch the other train that had our luggage before it left Penn Station. We had people make calls on their walkie-talkies to find out what track our original train was on. As soon as we got there we hurried to the track. We found the train. They had moved our luggage out to the hall in the train. Fortunately all of our luggage was there. Out of all that we learned that if your train is running late, don't get off!

I thought this trip was a good experience, especially helping people start a new school.

# 12
# Visit to an Alternative School and a Foundation

We needed to go into New York City to visit some schools and Josh Mailman, who was giving Jerry a grant for $20,000. We were with Patrice, who was from France. He had gone to a conference in Chicago with Jerry. He runs an association of alternative schools in France.

We went to the Mineola station to catch the Long Island Rain Road train. We didn't think that we would catch it, because we were very late. We pulled in just as the train pulled in. There was a parking space right there. Then all three of us were running for the train. because it just stopped. We just barely made it.

We took a subway over to the Barbara Taylor School. It was in an apartment building. There were sixty kids in the school, and even though there were very few kids, it seemed crowded because it was in a small area.

Barbara Taylor was the one who started the school. She wasn't there when we visited. Now she goes around talking about the school. So we talked to the woman who is the director of the school. She told us they use some kind of psychology or whatever, to run the school.

The school is in Harlem. The kids were mostly black and Hispanic, and there were some white kids.

After talking to the director for a while, we went in to talk to the older group. They were 11 to 13. I think there were nine of them. We ran a "question class" with them. A question class is where you think, and you ask any questions that you ever wanted to know to answer to. It doesn't matter how funny it is.

At first the kids weren't really responding, but after a while they were coming up with some of the craziest questions, like "How do bears clean their noses?" The most popular questions were "Why isn't Patrice speaking--does he speak English?", "Where do bell-bottoms come from?" and "Where do Jordan's come from?" We picked out the ones that everyone liked the best by having a show of hands. We wound up getting into a discussion about things like "How do you get someone's name, to endorse something, and how much do you pay them?" and "What kind of clothing or sneaker designs do you think people will like in the future?"

I thought that the kids were pretty smart, and had some control of what happened in the school, but I don't think they really used their control. They talked about one incident in which a teacher pushed a kid, and the kid pushed the teacher back, and the kid got suspended for a day, and they didn't do anything about the teacher. So the kids brought that up, and the teacher got put on probation for 30 days. Then

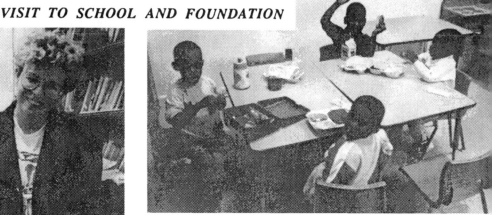

*Above: Some of the children at the Barbara Taylor School, in New York*
*Left: The director of the Barbara Taylor School*

the teacher quit on the second day. The reaction of the kids was that they really had some power and they were glad that the teacher had left.

What I thought was funny was that the kids said that they liked the school, but they didn't think that kids would ever go to school if they didn't have to, which made me think that it wasn't really a free school.

After seeing the school we went to see Josh Mailman. His office was in the second to the top floor of a very tall building. It was the 21st floor. It was on Park Avenue. The buildings in the area were tall and had interesting shapes. One of the buildings in that area was Trump Tower. Jerry made a joke about it and said it was now the IRS Tower.

We talked to Josh Mailman about alternative schools and the grant. I talked to him about the trip that we took to Montana to help them start a school. He was nice and he was pretty busy. He had one phone call after another, sometimes two at the same time. I've seen people doing that on TV, but I've never seen it in real life. He seemed interested in what we were doing.

After the meeting we went back to Penn Station to get the train. It was strange walking into Penn Station. It looked so bare after they've kicked out all the homeless people. I don't think it was right of them to kick them out. Now people can't see them laying around, and wouldn't realize that we have a problem, so that they can help. What I thought was nice was that there were people there representing the homeless and getting money for them. We made a contribution.

# 13
# Teen Trip to California

The trip that I went on to California was different in many ways from the one to Montana. On this trip I was with a group of kids, and a lot of the kids were not from alternative schools or homeschoolers, but from public school. I thought that might be a problem, because they weren't used to the way that Jerry did things with alternative schooling, like meetings, the stop rule, and other things. The stop rule is where a kid says "stop!" if he is getting seriously mad about something, and the other kid may not realize it. It avoids lots of fights.

One of the purposes of the trip for Jerry was going to a conference of public alternatives at Stanford University. Jerry decided to open the trip to the public, and parents would pay for their kids to go. He turned it into a travel camp. We were going to go by train, because it was more enjoyable and cost less money. After the conference we planned to travel all around California, going to Disneyland, Universal Studios, Hollywood, etc.

Eight people were on the trip. Two of the boys were from Huntington, Mike and John, and the third, Tosha, was from Virginia. The two other girls, Heidi and Lisa, were from Syosett. They were all thirteen. Then there were Jerry and Angela, the two leaders, well, sort of. I say "sort of" because everyone helped make the decisions, rather than them just telling us what we were going to do. Angela lives in Albany. She was a student in Jerry's school. She's 18, and she's been working at the Free School, in Albany.

We were going to catch the train at Grand Central Station in New York City. When we got there, we had one little problem: How do we carry our bags? Grand Central Station is a big place, and we had to walk all the way through it to find the people we had to meet there. I was finding all kinds of useful ways of carrying my bag. Of course, none of them worked for very long. I finally just decided to drag it along behind me. It kept banging into things and eventually tore my bag to shreds, but it was the best I could do.

Now, the first three of us were getting hungry, so we went to a pizza place in Grand Central. The kid who was with us didn't eat cheese, so we went to a place across from us to get him something and left our bags across the hall, about ten feet away. While we were eating, we kept checking on the bags to make sure nobody took them, because Grand Central Station was not the safest place to leave your bags. When we picked up our bags to get going and walked a little ways, the kid that was already with us, who had been carrying Jerry's video camera, realized that it was missing. We went to check if it might still be there, but it wasn't. We told a nearby security guard, and they kept on the lookout for it, but unfortunately, it wasn't found.  So we didn't have a video camera for the trip.

Everybody eventually showed up, and we got on the train. Right away we began to see how much fun the train could be. As soon as our tickets were collected we started exploring the train. I don't think any of the other kids had ever been on an AMTRACK train before (Long Island Railroad is barely a train).

One of the first things that they discovered was the lounge and snack bar, where we spent most of our (conscious) time. By about 9:30, everybody except us was out of the lounge car, and we had it all to ourselves.  We were all hanging out in there, and we had sort of a party. Then we had THE FIRST MEETING.

On the agenda for THE FIRST MEETING was 1. Rules 2. Caffeine  3. Bedtime.

I chaired the first meeting, because nobody really understood or cared who chaired the meeting, and Jerry, Tosha and I were the only ones who knew how to do it.  For the rules, we decided that we would try for consensus, but if we couldn't get consensus, we would do majority vote, and if the smaller half felt strongly enough, then could call a re-vote. Although he didn't like to, Jerry reserved the right to make emergency decisions.

Then we came to number two on the agenda: Soft drinks with caffeine. Jerry brought it up because he knew caffeine kept him awake, and it kept most other people awake. So he proposed that after a certain hour, we stop drinking anything with caffeine in it. There were many objections, arguments and revotes. But we finally decided that, for that night it would be the choice of the person who was drinking it. Some people claimed not to be kept awake by caffeine. So we thought we'd try it for that first night and see what happened. Unfortunately, almost everyone stayed awake. Maybe it was because of the caffeine, or maybe it was just because we were excited because it was the first night. Even though, the next day we decided that people couldn't have caffeine (cokes, etc) past 9 PM. We eventually all agreed.

Angela was not at that first meeting because we didn't pick her up until 11 PM when we got to Albany.

When we got to Chicago, we boarded the western train. Again we took a tour. The kids liked the fact that the western trains are double decker and have movies at night.

*Top:An interesting rock formation in Colorado*
*B: Lisa and Heidi on the train to California*

Going over a railroad trestle in Colorado

*Crossing the Colorado River on the train*

In the lounge we played card games, Jerry told stories, and he showed us something he called "the Gestalt Test", which is a test of your powers of observation. I'd tell you about it, but I don't want to give it away.

One of the funniest things on the trip was the way we cooked soup on the train. We would go downstairs to the bathroom, plug in Angela's teapot, and cook oriental soup in it. At one point we got kicked out and had to do it in the hallway. But it did save us money.

We went through Denver, Colorado, then went through the beautiful mountains and lots of tunnels. Later, it was up to 110 degrees in the desert, so the train had to slow down to 40 MPH because the tracks were expanding. We didn't realize it, because the train was air conditioned.

The train was very late getting to California, so they gave everybody on the train a free dinner in the diner.

Finally we got to Oakland. We were on the train almost three days. Jerry's friend Ken was there to pick us up in a minivan.

*Ken Lebensold in front of the Rent a Wreck*

We had to tie luggage on the roof. Lisa's luggage we nicknamed "the dog", or sometimes, "the cow" because it was so big that people always walked it around by a leash. Jerry told her to bring five changes of clothes, and she brought about 20!

That first night we stayed at Ken and Etta's. Jerry went over to pick up a Rent a Wreck van, which lived up to its name, but at least it worked.

Next was the conference, which wasn't the highlight of the trip for any of us, except maybe Jerry. It was a public alternative school conference, and it was at Stanford University.

There are mainly two kinds of alternative schools, "Choice" and "at risk". Choice schools are ones where children have a choice about going to the school and how to run it. They're for anybody that wants to go. At risk schools are for problem kids, like kids who have trouble learning.

Our workshop was to show how to use democracy. We had a meeting, and it was a real one, too. I thought that was funny that we showed them a real meeting. It was a small room, but there were more than 20 people watching. I guess they thought it was interesting. We also did a "question class" to try to figure out what everyone is most interested in.

That night we stayed at Dorothy's house. She made a video about alternative schools called "Why do these kids love school?" That was the best video. You figure it might be boring. It was interesting meeting the woman who actually made the video. It's going to be on television all over the country.

Angela was sick for at least the first half of the trip, so in the first half there isn't much tell about her, except that Jerry had to drive her back and forth to the doctor's. We had to be good because it was harder for Jerry. She was nice. She went to alternative schools and was brought up that way. She's unique, just different from anybody I've ever met. She's understanding. She knows how to help people. And she's tough, she can handle things. And she's only 18.

We took a day to go to San Francisco. Awesome! ..The cable cars, the buildings weren't just square shaped and the people were NOT New Yorkers.

The cable cars were cool. I thought they were going to be in the air. They ran on tracks pulled by an underground cable. The cars are very old, and you could stand up and hang on to the outside. When the first cable car came from the other direction we all looked in shock like Winston in Ghost Busters when the ghost train was coming toward him. The people hanging from the other cable almost hit us.

We went to Chinatown and looked in the stores and ate. Then we went on an outside elevator to the top of the Fairmont Hotel. The first feeling when you got on was WOW! Looking down on the whole city was really fun. We could point out the places we'd been and see the pyramid. After we got down, we decided to go up again. But that time, on the way down, some English guy pushed to "door open" button, so the elevator came to a stop, right where there were no floors, just cement wall. We were very high, just coming down from the top. Everybody got worried. Someone picked up the emergency phone, and they told him to push the little red button. But it was totally dark. We didn't know which little red button. Mike had a match and lit it so we could see. We found the button, pushed it, and finally we were on the way down. We hoped never to see that English guy again.

The next day we went on a cruise under the Golden Gate Bridge and we saw Alcatraz. It's a jail that they turned into a museum. It's the one David Copperfield broke out of. Then we went to Pier 39, Lisa and Heidi's highlight of the trip (because they LOVE shopping). Personally, I wouldn't know, because I spent the whole time in the arcade.

*Tosha (L), Heidi and Lisa (R), on the Bay Cruise*
*Below: Alcatraz Prison, in San francisco Bay*

We went back to the end of the conference, then we went over to Santa Cruz to stay with the John and Jeane Williams, Jerry's friends. They are Ba'hai's, and they lived at the Ba'hai' Center. It was nice. They had a pool, a dining room, ping pong table and lots of redwoods. Ba'hai's believe that there's just one God for all the religions.

*Tosha leaping into the pool
at the Bosch Ba'hai' School*

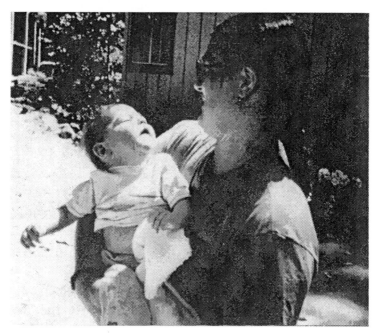

*Jeanne Williams holding Troy*

The Roller Coaster at the amusement park in Santa Cruz

We went down to the pier in Santa Cruz. There were supposed to be a lot of sea lions there, but there was only one fat, lazy sea lion, lying under the dock. The others were gone, migrating. After that we spent the day at an amusement park. It was amazing that it had survived the earthquake.

*At the amusement park in Santa Cruz*

One of the places we ate at was Sizzler. Nothing special, right? But it gets rather boring after going there twelve times. But it was the cheapest place we could find. You get a salad bar with a big selection, and the children's price is really cheap. If you're traveling with a large group of kids, I'd suggest it. Of course, I'm probably beginning to sound like some kind of used car salesman, so lets get on to another subject.

We left the Williams' and decided to see a redwood park nearby. Just as we got there, we heard a loud whistle. By, chance we happened to get there right as a steam train that toured the park was coming in. We decided to go on it and we saw some of the oldest and biggest redwood trees around. I think it's good to be able to do things when they happen. If

*A redwood forest near Santa Cruz,*

we had a schedule that we were locked into, we wouldn't be able to do a lot of things that we ended up doing.

We headed back toward San Francisco. On the way we saw a beach called Pebble Beach and decided to look around. It was rather different from any other beach that most of us had been to. There were interesting sandstone formations all along the shore. It wasn't like a sandy beach. If you stood on top of a tall rock fairly near the shore, you would get splashed as the waves came in and beat against the rocks.

That night we went to a baseball game, Giants versus Cardinals. It was at Candlestick Park. It was the first time I'd ever seen a major league baseball game! When it got darker, they turned on the lights. The lights were big, bright, and quite amazing. The Giants won. I guess home teams rarely lose. After the game, they had fireworks. They were some of the best fireworks I'd ever seen. They put music to it, and some Abraham Lincoln speeches.

Pictures we took at Pebble Beach
Below:Candlestick Park, day and night, with fireworks

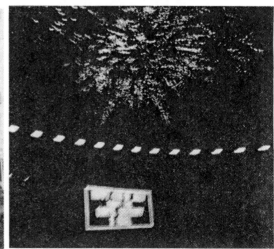

*This is us in front of the Exploratorium*

The next day we went to the Exploratorium in San Francisco. It's like a really big hands-on museum. I love museums, especially a hands-on science museum. That's got to be the ideal museum in the world for me. One of the things I liked best was a large pin screen, where you put your hand under it, and it comes out on top in the shape of your hand. I also liked the optical illusions center. In the sounds department, there was a place where you could talk into it, and it would say what you said backwards. So Jerry sang Row, Row, Row your Boat backwards into it, and it came out forward!

On our last day in San Francisco we went to Golden Gate Park and saw the Japanese Tea Garden. They had pagodas and weird bridges, and tiny trees, what do you call them? Bonsai? It was neat.

Then we went to the planetarium. I can't say anything special about it, because I've been to planetariums before, but I quite enjoyed it.

The Japanese Tea Gardens In Golden Gate Park

Jerry brought us back to Ken and Etta's house in Oakland, then went back to drop off the Rent a Wreck van.

In the morning, Etta's son, Steve brought us to the train in his mini van. This time we didn't have to tie anything to the roof because we brought out luggage to the train the day before. The train that we took from Oakland went to LA along the coast. I remember looking over the edge sometimes and saying, "Whoa, are we going to fall in the water?"

On the train I had a fight with Heidi over a pretzel that Mike gave me to share with Heidi. I started to break it in half, and Heidi grabbed it and said she wanted the whole thing, and claimed that I was going to have the whole thing. When I didn't give her the whole thing right away, she dumped a can of soda over my head, and that's when I got angry. She said she's wash my hair for me. I said I'd do it myself, but she still insisted on helping. We went down to the bathroom, and I started washing my hair, but she still insisted on helping, so I let her help dry it off, but I was still angry at her, and called a meeting. We finally settled it out. I talked for a long time after that to Jerry and some of the kids.

We got off the train at Los Angeles. When we got there we found out that the van that we rented wasn't there, so we all hung out at the train station until Jerry got it worked out. It wasn't too bad. We all had fun pushing each other on the luggage carts. Jerry was frantic, running around making phone calls. We ended up taking two cabs to a Howard Johnson's Hotel and spending the night there and picking up the van the next day. The van rental company took two days off the rental to pay for the hotel.

Now that we had a vehicle, we started looking for Play Mountain Place, the school where we were supposed to stay the night before. Play Mountain Place is a school that Jerry knew about. They gave us permission to sleep there.

We dropped our stuff off at Play Mountain Place and decided to go to Hollywood. Hollywood wasn't much like I thought it would be. I expected it to be all glamorous and sparkling, with all kinds of big signs. But basically what I saw was a place with stars on the sidewalk and a place where there were hand prints of the stars. It was not as clean as I pictured it.

After seeing Hollywood we drove right down to Santa Monica Beach. There was a big arcade there and an amusement park. I think they were both a rip off. The arcade, for instance: You paid a dollar and got three tokens, but most of the games were two tokens, so then you had to get some more. Some of them were fun, but I don't think they were worth that much money.

I remember almost making Tosha sick on an amusement park ride. There was a Ferris wheel, and there were cars on it that went upside down. Tosha and I went on it together. Mike and John were in another one. I saw someone spinning around. I couldn't get it to do that, but I did get it to go upside down. I could stand it, but Tosha was getting sick, and I think it got stuck. Tosha said he was getting sick, so the guy undid it. His face was red, and as soon as we turned right-side up his face turned white. He was OK after that. I'm not sure he was really sick. Maybe he was joking.

Then we went down to the beach, which was below the arcade. We went swimming.

*Me rinsing off at Santa Monica Beach*

Then we went back to Hollywood. We tried to get the group in to see the Laugh Factory, but we were too young. We needed to be 18 or over to get in because they served liquor. I thought that was stupid, but I guess they have their reasons.

After the Laugh Factory put down, we attempted to go up into the hills above Hollywood to see the homes of some of the actors and actresses. It was really nice up there. When you first looked off the edge of the hill, it was sort of frightening, because it was a long way down, but then when you got used to it, it was really neat, looking down on all the lights. The houses were all really big and very pretty. We passed a few signs that said "No Trespassing." "Keep out", "Beware" and other such things.

We had gotten tickets for a TV show called "Hold Everything" at the Chinese Theater (where the movie stars' hand prints are). They were free, because they wanted an audience. Maybe they needed a clapping section.

The TV show was fun, and we almost got on camera. It was a game show it which they had stars, and they had to guess if someone on a video was going to do something or not. I knew one of the actors. He was from the show "Just the Ten of Us." We watched the taping of three shows in a row. They encouraged us to stay for all three by handing out raffles at the end.

What I thought was funny was, in one of the tapings, when the host was coming out, he tripped on a rug and he fell down. So they had to start taping all over again. Another funny part was when the host was supposed to say, "In this video the focus is on the lady in red" and instead he said, "The focus is on the lady in bed", so they had to retape that section, too.

The next day we went to Malabu Beach. It is mainly a surfing beach, but at one end there is some good body surfing waves. Jerry went in wading, and we pushed him in.

Below:Getting into the cold water at Malabu

*Angela on the beach at Malabu,*
*with Heidi in back of her*

Then we went over to Venice Beach. When we got there it was getting dark, so we didn't go swimming, but we walked along the boardwalk and looked in different shops. Jerry's shirt was wet and it was getting cold, so he had to get a new shirt somewhere. He wanted to get the cheapest one possible. We went past a booth that had shirts that said, "Muscle Beach" on them. Jerry asked for the cheapest, which turned out to be a sleeveless muscle shirt, which definitely was not Jerry, but he got it anyway because it was only $2. I don't think he'll ever wear it again.

On the way back to the van, John yelled out, "Hey, that's Peg Bundy!" He was a fan of the Bundy's. She's on the TV show, "Married With Children". She was sitting on a bench with her boyfriend. We knew it was her, because while we were there a couple of people went up to get her autograph. We decided not to disturb her, because she was in the middle of kissing her boyfriend.

One of our biggest goals in the trip was to go to Disneyland. Finally that day arrived. The first thing Jerry did was take a picture of all of us.

In front of Disneyland

I liked Space Mountain the best, even though it wasn't as fast as I thought it would be. I love fast roller coasters, as well as looping roller coasters. I think I went on about half the rides there. We stayed until late. We watched a little of the electric parade from the ski ride. I got a front seat view of the fireworks, and they were pretty good.

*Below: Me and Angela heading into the Matahorn at Disneyland*

*TRIP TO CALIFORNIA*

On the last day in the Los Angeles area we went to Universal Studios. It's a place where they make movies.

When we got there we went to the Star Trek show then the Conan Show. Then we went on the tour. It was a lot of fun. They took us inside and showed us how they made different special effects in movies. They showed us around some of the sets that they used in movies like "Back to the Future II." After, we went to three shows, "Riot Act", "Animal Actors", and "Miami Vice."

*Top: The group in front of Universal Studios*
*Bottom: Universal Studies set where*
*they made Back to the future*

A "flash flood" at Universal Studios

After Universal, we went back to Play Mountain Place to get our stuff and to bring it to the train station.

The only real thing that happened on the way from Los Angeles to Texas was that we saw a little bit of Mexico when we went through El Paso.

The train station at Austin was a tiny little place. Everyone was fighting over one phone because they wanted to call people while Jerry went to pick up our rented van.

Greenbriar was located down an old country dirt road. My first impression was that it was just going to be woods and not much to it, but boy, was I wrong.

When I first saw the buildings it looked just like girl scout camp, the worst thing in my life, because it looked like a bunch of little cabins, buried in the woods. But I found out differently. They had a swimming pool, a trampoline, and a lot of nice kids. The weather was hot. It felt like over 100 degrees. So the first thing we did was go swimming.

*Some of the kids in the pool at Greenbriar*

*Me in the pool at Greenbriar*

Then we all discovered the trampoline, and spent a lot of time there. We did a lot of that until the end of the day. Like, I remember when I had to get out of the pool because it was getting dark out, and they had to "zap" the swimming pool with chlorine or some other chemical.

*Mike on the trampoline at Greenbriar*

## TRIP TO CALIFORNIA

I had never seen any place like Greenbriar before. It was unusual because people all worked together there, and they were all friends. They shared almost everything. They made us feel welcome there. It was just like we almost fit in there.

At one point on the trip I went through a period where I just wanted people to leave me alone, "Get out of my face", but at that point I wouldn't have minded staying at Greenbriar longer. I wasn't anxious to get home. Actually, I never get homesick.

We left Greenbriar and got on the train to Chicago. We went through Dallas, which had interesting architecture. In Chicago we had a few hours between trains.

It was finally my 11th birthday. It started out as the worst birthday ever. Because everything was going wrong: I had to spend it on a train, and almost lost $5 in the process. I made a bet with one of the kids that I thought was impossible for him to win, and he won. It was a card trick that he was doing. After he did it I remembered I knew the trick from magic class, which made me feel even worse, because I got suckered out on a trick that I knew. It was the trick where they bet you the next card they turn over will be your card, but they've already turned over your card. So you bet, and the dealer goes back and turns over your card again.

Then we had an argument because I said that I had my legs crossed, or something like that. Finally we got it settled and I said that I'd never make excuses about bets that I lost.

When we got to Chicago we went to the Sears Tower. It's known for being the tallest building the the world. From a distance it didn't look taller than the World Trade Center, but when you went up to the top and looked down it was amazing.

We couldn't find a decent place to go for my birthday, so we went to Burger King. Maybe I shouldn't put it that way, but at that time, that's how I felt.

*Jerry and me after I crowned him at Burger King*

We went back to the station and got on the train to New York. Nothing was really happening. We were all sitting around doing nothing, like seeing if we could drink coke without putting the can to our mouth. Then Tosha came to get me for a meeting. He said it was about cheating. So I went down to the lounge car for the meeting. Jerry sent me back and said to get the other girls. Then Tosha told me that the girls wanted to talk to me, and they talked to me about nothing.

Then we went back and started the meeting. Now the meeting was about nothing. I was beginning to wonder what this was all about.

Then, all of a sudden, a waiter walked down the aisle with a tray in his hand and a whole bunch of cake, singing "Happy Birthday"! Everybody yelled, "surprise!", and the whole lounge car started to sing. Then I figured that maybe the day wasn't so bad after all.

# 14
# Conclusion

Now that you've heard about all my trips and experiences, you can see that I've met a lot of new kids and made a lot of new friends through homeschooling. I'm saying this for those of you who may think that I didn't socialize enough through homeschooling, or get enough time with my peers. It's even easier to make new friends through homeschooling because the kids are basically friendlier. Maybe it's because they're not under so much pressure from all the unnecessary work in public school and always having to give in to their peers about being cool, and looking "stylish" and knowing who are the "cool" people to hang with.

One of the best aspects of my homeschooling was getting to travel, because learning while traveling sure beats sitting in an old classroom any time,or sitting around the house. The reason that I think it's better is because you get to have fun while you're learning. You get to explore the world and what it really is. In school they teach math on a piece of paper. But through my travels I got to experience how to use math in real life. Not only math, but just about anything else that I'll need for life; like how to understand people and get along, and how to use language in communication to make contact with people, how to help people with their problems, and how to solve problems. I also learned about current events and what's going on in the world.

    At this point, the book is starting to annoy me because it's starting to sound like one big advertisement for homeschooling. So I should try to think of something bad to say about it. .......................*Um*..............I can't think of anything bad about it. Sorry. I mean who could miss staying after school every day or being yelled at by the teacher?

    In this book I've given you some my homeschooling experiences and some of the ways that we did did things. But this isn't the way it has to be, because if you would like to start homeschooling, you should read other books and use your own ideas. I think that homeschooling is a good experience for both parents and children.

If you have any questions, call us or write to us at:

417 Roslyn Rd.
Roslyn Heights, NY 11577    (516 625-3257)

Since writing her book, Jenifer Goldman went on to graduate from an alternative high school on Long Island. She applied to and received a scholarship from Bel Rea Institute, from which she graduated with honors, becoming a licensed Veterinary Technician after passing her national boards. She is currently living in Colorado with her husband, Jonathan Judge, and a supervisor in a veterinary laboratory.

Breinigsville, PA USA
10 June 2010
239570BV00002B/2/A